JONAH

Len Jenkin

BROADWAY PLAY PUBLISHING INC
New York
www.broadwayplaypublishing.com
info@broadwayplaypublishing.com

Cover art by Len Jenkin

First printing: May 2018
I S B N: 978-0-88145-770-4

Book design: Marie Donovan
Page make-up: Adobe InDesign
Typeface: Palatino

JONAH was originally produced by Undermain Theatre in Dallas. The world premiere opened on 15 April 2016 with the following cast and creative contributors:

MARY MARGARET................................. Katherine Bourne
MR RHODES..Patrick Bynane
MR BONES ....Jeremy Schwartz
TERRI...Courtney Mentzel
DABBY...Marcus Stimac
JONAH...Jonathan Brooks
LADY J... Whitney Coulter
SHEILA .... Kelsey Milbourn
GOD/THE WHALE...Bruce DuBose

Director..Katherine Owens
Scenic design..John Arnone
Sound design..Bruce DuBose
Costume design.......................................Amanda Capshaw
Properties design...Linda Noland
Lighting design ....Steve Woods
Additional music......................Paul Semrad, Rob Menzel,
Bruce DuBose

NOTE ON MUSIC

For performance of copyrighted songs, arrangements
or recordings referenced in this play, permission
of the copyright owner(s) must be obtained. Other
songs, arrangements or recordings may be substituted
provided permission from the copyright owner(s) of
such songs, arrangements or recordings is obtained
or songs, arrangements or recordings in the public
domain may be substituted.

CHARACTERS & SETTING

MR RHODES AND COMPANY— AT THE HOUSE BY THE SHORE

MR RHODES, *a Bible scholar and professor*
MARY MARGARET, MR RHODES' *daughter*
DABBY, *a beach bum*

The Book of Jonah—ON LAND AND SEA

JONAH, *the reluctant prophet*
GOD
PIRATE QUEEN
PIRATES *(women)*
THE WHALE *(Leviathan)*
CRUISE PASSENGERS
PEOPLE OF NINEVEH

EVERYWHERE ELSE

"BLIND" MR BONES
SHEILA, *a night school student, and a singer*
HER BAND *(Sheila and the Love Tones)*
BARFLIES *at the Grass Skirt Grill*
TERRI, A CASHIER
WANDA, A BARMAID

"For thou hadst cast me into the deep, in the midst of the seas…all thy billows and thy waves passed over me.
The waters compassed me about, even to the soul…
The Book of Jonah, K J V

"If everything seems under control, you're not going fast enough."
Mario Andretti

(Begin...)

(MR RHODES, at his desk in his house by the sea. Scholarly tomes, papers, ancient artifacts. A candle is lit.)

(His daughter, MARY MARGARET, is nearby.)

MR RHODES: From Edward Lane, "Arabian Society in the Middle Ages", Longmans Greene and Company, London, 1883.

One obscure Sufi sect preaches that the earth was unstable, and therefore God created an angel of great size and strength to go beneath and place it on his shoulders. But there was no support for the angel's feet, so God created Nergal, a giant bull with a thousand eyes, and ordered this bull to go beneath the angel, and he bore him on his back. But there was no support for the bull. Therefore God created an enormous fish that no one could look upon because of its vast immensity and the flashing of its eyes, and God commanded the fish to be a support for the bull. The name of this fish is Leviathan.

MARY MARGARET: *(Softly)* Leviathan.

MR RHODES: God placed, as Leviathan's support, the ocean, and under the ocean, darkness—

MARY MARGARET: Dad? Dad?

MR RHODES: ...and the knowledge of mankind can never know the nature of that darkness.

MARY MARGARET: Dad? It's time for our walk.

MR RHODES: Give me one more minute...

MARY MARGARET: Dad…

MR RHODES: All right. Jonah will keep. (*He stands, blows out his candle.*) Mary Margaret, let's hit the beach.

(MARY MARGARET *and* MR RHODES *are gone.*)

(MR BONES *on the road. He walks along the shoulder of a two-lane blacktop. Dusty, travel worn, with dark glasses, a white cane with a red tip.*)

MR BONES: I don't mind if you stare at me.
Or if you look away.
I'm a sorry spectacle. A human being at the back end of bad luck.
(*He looks over the audience.*)
Don't worry about me.
Not that you would. There's so little kindness in the world these days. So little charity.
I happen to have found a ten dollar bill on the floor of the men's room at that Sunoco up the road.
Fortunate.
I have the price of a drink, so I'm on my way to the Grass Skirt Grill. I'm an habitue.
But first, some dinner.
Perhaps a large box of Jujubees.
Hoo! Hooo!

(*The Convenience Store appears.* TERRI, THE CASHIER GIRL.)

CASHIER GIRL: Circle K. Soft drinks, cigarettes, phone cards, coffee, slushees, Slim Jims, hot dogs, gum, chips. Gas.

(MR BONES *heads in the wrong direction.*)

CASHIER GIRL: Over here.

(MR BONES *turns, comes toward* CASHIER GIRL.)

MR BONES: Gimme a large box of Jujubees.

CASHIER GIRL: You got it.

(CASHIER GIRL *holds out the Jujubees to* MR BONES.)

CASHIER GIRL: Candy's right in front of you.
One ninety-five.

MR BONES: *(Taking Jujubees)* Fucking robbery.
Overcharge a man for his Milky Way.

CASHIER GIRL: You got Jujubees.

MR BONES: Shame, a beautiful girl like you, stealing
from the blind.
It's true what they say.

CASHIER GIRL: What do they say?

MR BONES: The red hand of the devil spins the world.
(*He wanders away from the store, opening his candy.*)
Hoo! Hooo!

OWL: *(O S)* Hoo! Hooo!

(MR BONES *looks up, finding the source of the cries.*)

MR BONES: Owl. They love jujubees.

(MR BONES *tosses a jujubee high in the air. Sound of an owl
snatching a jujubee out of the air. Swoosh as the* OWL *flies
off.*)

OWL: *(O S)* HOOO!

MR BONES: Hooo!
I have a romantic inspiration…
(*He makes his hesitant way back to the convenience store.*)

CASHIER GIRL: I'm over here.

(MR BONES *approaches* CASHIER GIRL.)

MR BONES: Do you know who I am?

CASHIER GIRL: Yep. You're one more fucked up old
man.

MR BONES: I'm Mister Bones.

CASHIER GIRL: I don't give a shit what your name is.

MR BONES: I love you. Come away with me. Old
Algiers! A tropic isle!

CASHIER GIRL: Get out of here or I'm calling the
manager.

MR BONES: I am the Manager.
You'll remember Mister Bones when the world goes
dark and the Black Wind seeps in under your door.
I'm leaving now, with my heart broken.
We'll meet again.
It's been a pleasure.

(MR BONES *wanders off, as the* CASHIER GIRL *takes out her
cell, dials.*)

CASHIER GIRL: Bobby? ...Bobby, it's me... Too many
creeps today...I'm O K... Not until eight...

MR BONES: (*From a distance, O S*) Hoo! Hoo!

CASHIER GIRL: No, I want to talk to you... Bobby,
don't ask me to do that. It's weird up there.... If the
homeless dude in the belfry.... Jonah, whatever. If
he owes you fifty, get it your own damn self. He's
your customer.... I know, I know you're going out
of business..... I still fucking insist. All I need is you
in jail. Bobby, ask Chino or Pepsi to... O K, O K. I'll
be your fucking bill collector. But if I get raped and
murdered, its your fault.... Definitely. From the Dairy
Queen. Queenburger, large fries, vanilla shake. Super
thick.... That's it. Extra ketchup. And Bobby, I need to
talk to you.... Not on the phone. It's important... O K,
O K. See you later.... Yeah, I love you too.

(*Walking along a highway near the beach,* MR BONES.)

MR BONES: I'm late. Sheila and the Love Tones come on
at nine.

(MR RHODES *and his daughter* MARY MARGARET *appear in the distance.*)

(Sound of surf, gulls)

(MARY MARGARET *sings. Suggested song:* Diamond in My Crown. *Continuing under:*)

MR BONES: Ah! It's Mr Rhodes and his daughter Mary Margaret, strolling by the seaside.
In the gloaming.

(MARY MARGARET *sings. Continuing under:*)

MR BONES: Brilliant man. A professor of Biblical Studies.

(Suddenly MR RHODES *staggers…)*

MR RHODES: AAAHHHHH! AHHH!
(He falls to the sand. He's twitching, shuddering.)

MR BONES: A blood vessel bursts in his brain—he's having a stroke.

(MARY MARGARET *tries to sit him up—she can't.*)

MR BONES: His eyes are open, pupils dilated, seeing nothing.
At last, he's still.
The surf rolls in over him.
Mary Margaret wont leave him, not even to get help.
She sits by him through the night, makes drawings in the sand that the sea washes away.

(Sunrise)

(DABBY, *the local beach bum and* MR RHODES' *handyman, is searching the surfline for driftglass.*)

(He takes one look at MR RHODES *and* MARY MARGARET, *pulls out his cellphone.*)

DABBY: *(On cell)* I need an ambulance…

*(The light fades on the three of them—*DABBY *on the phone,* MARY MARGARET, *and the still body of* MR RHODES.*)*

MR BONES: An hour after they wheel Mr. Rhodes into the hospital they drill three neat holes in his skull. Brain surgery. He's in the hospital for a month. He's back home now. At his house on the beach. Healing.
The mind's a funny thing…

(Music. The Grass Skirt Grill. WANDA's *the barmaid.* SHEILA *and her band onstage. The band plays under…)*

BAND MEMBER: Aloha.
Welcome to the Grass Skirt Grill. We're Sheila and the Love Tones—every Thursday night.
Join us.

(The band plays on, and SHEILA *sings an oldie.)*

(Suggested song: You Belong To Me*)*

SHEILA: *(Sings. Continuing under:)*

(There's an obnoxious drunk at a table. It's JONAH, *contemporary clothes. A large drink in a coconut is in front of him. As* SHEILA *sings, he mumbles and shouts, to himself and everyone around.)*

JONAH: Bunch of drunks and losers…on the run again…
Vaya no Dios, baby…
I'm invisible. Invisible man!
Ocean…fucking squids…

*(*SHEILA *ends her number. A smattering of applause)*

JONAH: I belong to me, that's who, do what I damn… please…

SHEILA: Thank you so much. Love you all. *(Blows kisses to the audience)* We'll be right back…

(The band plays quietly as SHEILA *ducks off behind a fishing net hung with shells and tiki gods. She dials on her cell, listens.)*

(No answer)

SHEILA: Fuck him.
(She dials again, listens. Again, no answer.)
The son of a bitch hasn't picked up for a week.

*(*MR BONES *arrives, feels his way to the bar.)*

WANDA: *(To* MR BONES*)* The usual?

MR BONES: Indeed. Zombie skullpuncher with a twist.

SHEILA: One more try.
(She dials her cell again.)
Who is this? What? I can't hear....
(The connection must be lousy, voices unintelligible...)
(She puts away her phone.)
Line's dead.
Maybe that was the daughter. He said he had one, I think.
I gotta get out there to see him. Face to face. Better that way.
(She looks over the crowd at the bar.)
Maybe one of these assholes will give me a ride.

WANDA: *(Shouting)* Which one of you assholes has the red Porsche 360, the ragtop? Move it! You're blocking the driveway.

(Nobody responds.)

JONAH: Fucking nerve. So much rudeness in the world these days.

MR BONES: It's a plague.
You must be Jonah. I'm Mr Bones.

JONAH: Mr Brains, the sonofabitch who owns that car oughta be arrested. 'Lectric chair. Fry the bastard.

SHEILA: That red Porsche is yours.
Isn't it?

JONAH: Goddamn right it is. What's it to you?

SHEILA: Maybe I better help you move it before Wanda
calls a towtruck.

JONAH: I need another drink first. They make a nice
Zombie skullpuncher at the Grass Skirt.

MR BONES: *(Lifting his drink)* Indeed they do.

*(The Zombie skullpunchers are in coconuts, with death's
heads painted on, and paper umbrellas.)*

BAND MEMBER: *(Raising his own skullpuncher)* Aloha.

JONAH: Shut up.
I've had a few. Somebody's following me, and he can't
find me if I'm drunk enough.

SHEILA: He's not gonna find you. You're with me now.

*(SHEILA manages to get JONAH on his drunken feet, get one
arm of his over her shoulder.)*

JONAH: With you? Where we going?

SHEILA: All my friends are alcoholics. I know how to
take care of you.

JONAH: You a working girl?

SHEILA: You wish. Let's get outta here. What's your
name?

JONAH: Jonah.

SHEILA: I'm Sheila.

JONAH: I need to get to Joppa.

SHEILA: Jonah, gimme your car keys.

(SHEILA wrestles the keys out of JONAH's pocket.)

(In the Porsche)

(JONAH *tries to stagger in on the driver's side but* SHEILA *shoves him into the passenger seat.*)

SHEILA: I'll drive.

(SHEILA *does. Deep throated roar of the Porsche. They're gone.*)

(MR RHODES, *in his house by the sea.* MARY MARGARET *and* DABBY. *Late at night.* MR RHODES *is propped up in a chair, his expression vacant, uncomprehending. His head lolls to one side.* MARY MARGARET *reads to him from his own handwritten notes on a yellow pad. She's hoping for a response, some recognition.* DABBY *watches them.*)

MARY MARGARET: *(Reading)* These seafarers were probably Ninevites—worshipped the great bull, Nergal. Nergal.

MR RHODES: Ah…ah…unnh…

(And silence)

MARY MARGARET: *(Reading)* Human sacrifice was no news to them. Jonah was probably lashed to the helm before they threw him into the sea. Open parenthesis—the great wheel of the helm is the wheel of Vitru… Vitri…

DABBY: Vitruvius. Proportion. The circle of a man's life.

MARY MARGARET: Where do you pick up this stuff?

DABBY: I've got a library card.

MARY MARGARET: Dad? Dad?

DABBY: The endless wheel of our spinning world.

MARY MARGARET: Dad, can you hear me?

(No response)

MARY MARGARET: *(Reading again)* In the end these pagan sailors throw Jonah into the sea. But first they pray as the storm rages, delaying, risking their own lives. They don't know there's a whale below. They think they're about to murder him to save themselves. They each call on their own dark gods—Ba'al, Ishtar, Tammuz—and other gods whose names are forgotten. "Oh, Lord, lay not upon us innocent blood."

(No response from MR RHODES. *His head lolls, and his eyes are empty.)*

DABBY: His own words. It was worth a try.

MARY MARGARET: It's what he loves…
(She's sobbing.)

DABBY: Makes no difference.
Not yet.

*(*DABBY *goes to* MARY MARGARET, *puts an arm around her, comforts her as she cries.)*

DABBY: Like the neurologist said, it's gonna take time…

*(*JONAH's *car, rolling.* SHEILA *is at the wheel. He has his bottle, drinks.)*

JONAH: Drive me to Joppa. As the fly crows. Metal to the pedal. Hammer down.
Drive it like I stole it.

SHEILA: Did you?

JONAH: Did I what?

SHEILA: Steal this fancy ass car.

JONAH: How else would I get it?
I think, just maybe, I've been on this road before. In a haywagon.
Or a bus.
Joppa's by the sea, you know that?

SHEILA: I've never been to…

JONAH: *(Sings)*
By the sea,
by the sea,
by the beautiful sea,
you and me,
you and me,
oh how happy we'll....
I'm gonna buy a ticket. Cash money. Got just enough.
Ticket on a ship.

SHEILA: You taking a cruise or something?

JONAH: Zactly. A cruise or something. Joppa's a big
port. Yacht or an ocean liner or a fucking rowboat...

SHEILA: Jonah, you're a lucky guy.

JONAH: If I get any luckier, someone'll come up behind
me and cut my throat.

SHEILA: Uh-uh. You're with me now. I got you covered.

JONAH: Actually, you don't know shit about my
situation.
God wants me to..

SHEILA: Shut up with the God crap. I've got enough
headaches without your spiritual fantasy life.
Have another drink.

(JONAH does, and another.)

SHEILA: Hey, God teach you anything about the Old
Testament?

JONAH: Are you making fun of me?

SHEILA: All those books, Genesis on down to Malachi.
I took a college course in that once, night school. My
friend, he was the professor.

JONAH: Who?

SHEILA: This guy I'm going to see. Don't worry, it's a
quick stop. He's by the ocean, right up the coast from

Joppa. Won't answer his phone, and I got something I
need to talk to him about…

JONAH: Hey, you're doing over eighty.

SHEILA: So? Enjoy the ride.

JONAH: Slow it down. I gotta keep moving. We could
get pulled over. Arrested.

SHEILA: We get locked up, you can always get your
mother a visitor's pass.

JONAH: My mother's dead. I'm an orphan.

SHEILA: I'm crying here.
You ever think you were in love with someone, and….

JONAH: Sheila, your love life is unimportant. And
boring.
Shut up and listen. I need to tell someone, anyone.
You'll do.
I was minding my own business and God appeared.
Uninvited.

(The car and SHEILA *are gone.)*

(Angelic background singing, and GOD *appears. He has a
ragged white robe, very tall. A medieval Mystery Play God.)*

GOD: Jonah? Jonah? Jonah!
There's a wrong note in the buzz buzz buzz of the bees,
the peppermint trees, the harmony.
JONAH! You out there?

(A church belfry)

JONAH: I'm here, Lord.
In this abandoned church. Next to the Jack In The Box.
Up in the belfry.
I don't know how I got here.
The bells are gone.
There's a window I can look through and see the stars,
cold as usual. I'd move, but I don't have the $29.95 for

the Traveler's Inn.
Or the cash to pay Bobby, my…

GOD: Enough.
You owe me, Jonah.

JONAH: That's bullshit. I don't…

GOD: You know damn well you owe me. You had the
Cavaliers in six.

JONAH: I never bet on basketball.

GOD: You think you can lie to me? Do I need to call
Louie?

JONAH: There's no need to call Louie.

GOD: He'll miss you. He's already weeping into his
Calvados.

JONAH: Can't you find some other sucker to…

GOD: You have business. In Nineveh.

JONAH: The people of Nineveh are nothing to me.
It's always the wrong end of winter there, buildings
blackened by fire, covered in layers of graffiti.
Squatters in the rubble, the last survivors of a defeated
army, clothes and bodies stinking, starved, stoned as
they can get.
I've seen a young girl in Nineveh, sprawled against
a door, stone dead, still holding a baby to her chest,
bawling its little lungs out.

GOD: I see you know the place.

JONAH: A cousin of mine runs a penny arcade behind
City Hall.

GOD: Don't waste time playing ski-ball.
It's a prophecy job.
The whole city is an evil circus. A twenty-four seven
pervert party. You can see the neon from nearby star
systems. Worst of all, Ninevites worship Nergal,

that idiotic bull with a thousand eyes, and they put a
furnace in his belly for the children they throw in to
keep him happy. The children scream as they burn.
Give them forty days. Or forty nights. Whatever. When
time's up, they all DIE.

JONAH: Everybody dies.

GOD: Not like this. Fire. Flood. Plague.

JONAH: I'm on my way.

GOD: You better be. (*He disappears.*)

(MR BONES, *dark glasses, cane, bus driver's hat.*)

MR BONES: Jonah doesn't go to the penny arcade
behind City Hall. He doesn't go to Nineveh at all. As
usual, he flees from God's wrath—
This time, he hops a bus.

(*Sitting in the back of the bus is* MR RHODES. JONAH,
*nervous, on the run, looking over his shoulder, gets on
board.*)

(MR RHODES, *his head lolling, clearly ill, watches* JONAH.)

MR BONES: Non-stop for Joppa, that charming town
by the sea. I'm your driver, Mr Bones. Keep your arms
and legs in the vehicle at all times. No smoking, eating,
or spitting.

(JONAH *sneaks a sandwich out of his pocket, begins to
unwrap it.*)

MR BONES: Jonah, put that meatball sub away, or I'll
have to ask you to deplane.

(MR BONES *takes the wheel of the bus, adjusts his dark
glasses.*)

(*Off they go.*)

MR BONES: (*Sings*)
Above, they say, is where we go, Where we go, where
we go…

Along the starry path we go
Along the Milky Way....
Relax, Jonah. After all, you're getting the ride for free.
It's on the house.

JONAH: What house?

MR BONES: We're all unfaithful servants, Jonah. Same
road, only difference is the scenery.
Instructive.
Ah, there's a Yogurt Barn, a nail salon, Mama Wong's
Vietnamese Cuisine, DoNut Hut, Walgreen's— "Free
Flu Shot," a Hobby Lobby...

(Screech of brakes)

MR BONES: JOPPA! Get off the bus!

(The bus and MR RHODES *are gone.)*

*(The docks at Joppa are full of drunken partying cruise
passengers.)*

(Music)

(Dance)

(They all dance up the gangplank of the huge cruise ship...)

CARNIVAL CRUISE SPOKESPERSON: *(On mike)* All aboard
the Carnival Princess, making port at San Juan, Saint
Thomas, McComb, Montevideo, and points west. All
aboard! *(To* JONAH*)* Ticket?

JONAH: What's the furthest destination?

CARNIVAL CRUISE SPOKESPERSON: *(On mike)* Tarshish.
Its at the far end of the world.

JONAH: One for Tarshish.

*(*JONAH *boards. Right behind him is* MR BONES, *in a
Hawaiian shirt.)*

MR BONES: Fortunately, I found a ticket for this Carnival Cruise just lying on the floor of the men's room in that Gulf QuikStop, right up the road.

(*All are on board. A moment of silence*)

MR BONES: And from the now deserted wharf, the uncheered ship for Tarshish, all careening, glides into the sea.

(*Engines, and a huge splash, and the Carnival Princess heads away from shore, growing smaller and smaller. It's gone.*)

(*Dead whale on the beach, but this one died long ago. Nothing but bones. DABBY's built a shelter out of the largest bones, leaning them together and throwing a tarp over them. He's been living there. Empty pizza box. Beer bottles. A bedroll. A clear jar full of driftglass. A blanket covers the sand. Cozy. DABBY and MARY MARGARET*)

MARY MARGARET: Dabby—some of Dad's pills are missing. Pain meds.

DABBY: Yeah?

MARY MARGARET: Did you steal them?

DABBY: No.

(MARY MARGARET *laughs at* DABBY.)

MARY MARGARET: Yes you did.
Tell the truth or I'm not going to see you anymore. You can squat in this arch of whale bones all by yourself till Kingdom Come.

DABBY: When you put it that way…I took them. I was feeling like shit one morning, and my old habit came back. Just once.

MARY MARGARET: Are you lying to me again?

DABBY: I'm telling you the truth.

MARY MARGARET: If we keep giving you the run of
the house, am I gonna find more of Dad's pain pills
missing?

DABBY: Never again, Mary Margaret.
It was just a few. I would never have taken them if
I thought your Dad would be without. My financial
situation has prevented certain journeys of the
imagination.
I missed it. I fucked up. I'm sorry.

MARY MARGARET: I forgive you, Dabby.
Don't ever lie to me or anyone in my family. Save the
lying for the rest of the world.

DABBY: I never told you, Mary Margaret. I've got a
kind of history of bad behavior. In my third year at
Princeton I…

MARY MARGARET: You went to Princeton?

DABBY: Harvard didn't take me. I liked it there.
Good grades, lit major. I was on the swimming team.
Butterfly.

MARY MARGARET: I want to go to college someday.

DABBY: You should. You will.

MARY MARGARET: Ever since Mom died, I've been the
only one…taking care of Dad, I mean. He needed me,
and so I stayed. I love him, and I love it here by the
ocean, but I always thought, someday soon, I'd go.
Now he's sick.
Princeton's gonna have to wait for me.

DABBY: I wasn't ready for it. In my junior year, a small
black cloud appeared on campus. I left under it.
My weakness for downers. And I was selling.
I'm a dropout, but I dropped myself out. Since then,
I've done every kind of work. I cut up junk cars with a
torch in New Mexico, mopped out on the night shift at

the Dallas Bus Depot. My last job was packing apples
in Yakima. Up in Washington. Hard labor, twelve
hours a day. They put me and the Mexicans in this
actually abandoned motel. Filthy sheets, rusted sink
dripping non stop. One night I took some pills and a
big green luna moth was circling the ceiling light and
talking to me. He said "You'll die in this place, Dabby.
Go to the ocean."
I retired and hit the beach. Odd jobs, hand to mouth.
Helping out your Dad.

MARY MARGARET: And searching for driftglass.
*(She reaches into DABBY's driftglass jar, takes out a few,
sifts them from hand to hand.)*
The blue ones are the eyes of drowned sailors.

DABBY: And the red ones?

MARY MARGARET: Those are bits of fire that flew off the
devil as he fell to earth. They hit the ocean with a hiss,
and drifted down to the bottom of the sea. Every now
and then a few wash up on shore.

(A long silence between them.)

DABBY: You know something, Mary Margaret? I get
nervous that somewhere nearby is a guy with a suit on,
stepping out of a shiny Lexus, talking on a cellphone.
That sonofabitch runs the world.

MARY MARGARET: Not my world.

DABBY: You know something else, Mary Margaret. I'm
in love with you.

(MARY MARGARET laughs.)

*(Then she gets up, replaces the driftglass, brushes sand off
herself.)*

MARY MARGARET: I need to get home. Dad may need
me.

DABBY: I need to have another look on his computer.
I'll come with you. That is, if you don't think I'll pocket
the silverware.

MARY MARGARET: All right then, Dabby.
Let's go.

(Music. At sea)

*(The ballroom on the Carnival Princess. Dancing, drinking.
In the crowd, unsteady and halting, MR RHODES. He
watches JONAH.)*

*(JONAH is at the bar. Nearby, MR BONES. He watches the
dancers circle the dancefloor.)*

MR BONES: See the wheel turn, and turn again. The
celestial bodies in their orbits, whirling around the
dark dancefloor for a million years. Planets, spiral
galaxies—a waltz across the firmament to the music of
the spheres.
Wheels in wheels.
(Exiting, to himself)
Just a wandering star…just a wandering star…

*(An elegant woman in a very tight dress approaches
JONAH.)*

PIRATE QUEEN: Hello, Slick.

JONAH: Hi. Uh, this your vacation?
You like the ocean?
Waves and fish and everything?
Uh, where you from?
I'm…

PIRATE QUEEN: Skip the small talk. I already like
you. You look completely out of place here, like you
wandered in out of another story altogether.

JONAH: I did. I'm fleeing. I should be in Nineveh,
standing on the steps of City Hall, preaching to…

PIRATE QUEEN: Tell it to someone who cares.
I'm a pirate.

PIRATES: *(O S)* Yo ho! Yo ho!

PIRATE QUEEN & PIRATES: *(Sing Blood Red Roses)*
Daddy was a shark who walked like a man
Go down, you blood red roses, go down
Mama was a singer in a mission band
Go down, you blood red roses, go down
Oh you pinks and posies

I run full sail when the wind is strong

Go down, you blood red roses, go down
Race the moonlight all night long
Go down, you blood red roses, go down

You can believe what the fuck you like
Go down, you blood red roses, go down
God's a whirlwind in the night
Go down, you blood red roses, go down
Go down.

PIRATE ONE: Why don't you all go fuck yourselves.

PIRATE QUEEN: A pirate queen, actually.

JONAH: You're putting me on.

PIRATE QUEEN: You think I'd bother? I don't need to lie
to anyone about anything. Not anymore.
Buy me a drink.

JONAH: Uh, O K. What are you…

PIRATE QUEEN: A Zombie skullpuncher. With an olive.

JONAH: That's my drink too! I drink skullpunchers all
the time.

PIRATE QUEEN: What a coincidence.

JONAH: Two Zom…

(Three skullpunchers, in their coconuts, appears instantly in the hands of MR BONES. *He hands two to* JONAH, *who hands one to the* PIRATE QUEEN.)

(All three sip.)

JONAH: You were saying?

PIRATE QUEEN: Oh, yeah. My pirates. We've taken over the ship. Chucked the Captain and all the officers overboard. To the sharks. We cut their nuts off first.

JONAH: You what?

PIRATE QUEEN: You should have heard them screaming. These passengers have no idea. As long as the food keeps coming, and the band keeps playing, they won't notice that the Pirate Queen is now running the show.

PIRATES: Yo ho! Yo ho!

PIRATE QUEEN: Our plan is to turn this ship into a floating casino and moor it in the Tarshish Lagoon. There's a sucker born every minute.

(The band strikes up.)

PIRATE QUEEN: Do you dance?

(They do. The PIRATE QUEEN *has amazing moves.* JONAH *barely manages to keep up.)*

(At the house by the sea. MR RHODES *sits quietly in a chair.* MARY MARGARET *prepares to shave him—a towel, shaving cream, a razor, a basin of water.* DABBY *is on* MR RHODES' *computer. Now and then, he watches the shaving.* MARY MARGARET's *every movement is gentle and careful. She drapes a towel around her father's neck. She steps in front of him, dabs some shaving cream on her own face to show him what she's about to do. No response. She lathers his face. She shaves him. She rinses his face clean with a damp cloth, then dries him.)*

MARY MARGARET: This morning he sat up by himself.
On the edge of the bed. I found him sitting there.

DABBY: The doctors at the hospital said, they said with
this kind of stroke, all his physical stuff will come
back soon. His brain is rewiring itself. All those little
neurons re-connecting.

MARY MARGARET: He can almost stand without help.
He couldn't do that two days ago.

DABBY: Its the speech center. Still a mess. And who
knows what he hears when we talk to him.
Everything is still scrambled or dead in there.

(DABBY *picks up a copy of the children's book,* Toad On
The Road, *hands it to* MARY MARGARET.)

DABBY: Try again with Toad. I tried last night. Got
nowhere.
He does best with you.

(MARY MARGARET *sits by her father, opens* Toad on the
Road.)

MARY MARGARET: Toad on the Road. Can you say that,
Dad. Toad on the road. Toad. Toad.

(*No response from* MR RHODES. *She reads to him, slowly
and gently.*)

MARY MARGARET: I love to drive, I am a toad
Here I come, toad on the road!
Hands on the wheel… Can you say wheel, Dad. Wheel.

(*Then suddenly…*)

MR RHODES: Hast done as it pleased thee so they took
up Jonah O Lord and cast forth…

(*And silence*)

MARY MARGARET: Dad. I heard you. Its me, Mary
Margaret. I heard you.

I know you're in there.
Talk to me. You've got to try.

MR RHODES: The wares in the ship are in the sea, O
sleeper arise, what shall we do, and cried every man
unto his god came unto Jonah the son of cry against
it for their wickedness is wickedness is wickedness.
Is come up before with them unto Tarshish from
the presence of the great wind take me up Tarshish
Tarshish what meanest thou.
And cast him forth and the sea ceased from her raging
the Lord exceedingly and there was a mighty tempest
that great city I am an Hebrew. And I fear to lighten it
of them but Jonah was gone down into the sides of the
ship why hast thou done this O sleeper arise and cast
me forth from the presence. So shall the sea be calm
unto you for I know that for my sake my sake my sake
the lot fell upon Jonah. Which hath made the dry sea
and the land were the men exceedingly afraid. Drive
Toad and cast lots unto Tarshish because he had told
them and made vows prepared to swallow up Jonah.

(Silence)

MARY MARGARET: Dad, can you say what I say?

(MR RHODES nods slightly.)

MARY MARGARET: I love you, Mary Margaret. I miss
you.

MR RHODES: O sleeper arise and the belly of hell three
nights and three nights and fast asleep shipmaster for
their wickedness great wind into the sea came to him
unto Nineveh. Lay not upon us innocent blood for
thou sacrifice unto Toad road for whose cause this evil
is upon us cast him forth cast him forth what is thine
occupation? Whence comest great wind into the sea
and of what people art thou?

MARY MARGARET: Dad, say Hello, Mary Margaret. I love you.

MR RHODES: Arise O sleeper. That we perish not.

(A long silence between the three of them.)

DABBY: I'll get his soup. Split pea.

MARY MARGARET: I know what he's trying to say. He's trying to say "I'm in here. Come find me."

(Somewhere else in America, the CASHIER GIRL *dials her cell.)*

CASHIER GIRL: *(On phone)* It's me…. He wasn't up in that church belfry. He's gone, that's all…. Door was open. I walked right in. Looked like no one had been there for days. Just a dirty blanket, half a rotting Subway sandwich…. Meatball. And three empty bottles of Jose Cuervo…
Bobby, just shut up for minute, O K? What I want to tell you is I'm late…. My period's late…. Of course I did…. Yeah…two months now. I didn't want to say anything cause I wasn't sure what….
Damn right its yours. Who else's would it be? Chino's? …Yeah… Yeah… That's up to you now, isn't it? … What's my Mom got to do with it? …Shut the fuck up with that. She did a shit job of raising me, and she screwed up my brother Jimmy's head. You think I'd… You what? …What?…
Bobby, that is so so stupid. Some guy with a headrag is gonna put a bullet in your brain, and my baby's not gonna have a Daddy….
Look, I gotta get back to work. We need to talk about this later, O K? …Yeah…yeah… Love you too. Bye.

(She's gone.)

(JONAH's *Porsche rolling through the night,* SHEILA *at the wheel.* JONAH *takes another drink from his bottle.*)

(SHEILA *dials her cell as she drives, listens.*)

SHEILA: No answer. Again. He's at a Biblical Studies Conference in Singapore. Or he's not answering the phone.
Or he's dead.
(She throws her cellphone out the car window.)

JONAH: Pirate queen…I went down…my stateroom, C deck….

(JONAH *pauses in his tale, tries to take another drink, falls over against the car door instead.* SHEILA *elbows him, and he sits up a bit straighter.*)

JONAH: Maybe this time, this time I'll make it..I'll get there…

SHEILA: Get where?

JONAH: Tarshish. Beautiful metropolis…

SHEILA: Tarshish. Where the fuck is that?

JONAH: End of the world.

SHEILA: You know something? I like you. You're a more interesting guy than the usual bozos I run into.

(SHEILA *tries to play the radio. Music, then only harsh static. She shuts it off.*)

SHEILA: Radio's dead. Talk to me.
You married?

JONAH: No.

SHEILA: Got a girlfriend?

JONAH: No.

SHEILA: *(Taking out a cigarette)* Got a light?

(JONAH *fumbles for a match, finds one, lights her cigarette. Silence between them)*

SHEILA: Say something else.

JONAH: Is there, uh, something particular you want me to say?

SHEILA: Anything that's not delusional shit about god and pirate queens. Something kind and thoughtful. About the stars. Crows over the wheatfield...
I know. Ask me to make love to you.

JONAH: Now? This car doesn't.. no back seat. Also, I might be a little drunk, and I...

SHEILA: Not now. Later tonight, after I take care of some business.

JONAH: You don't want to get involved with me.

SHEILA: Don't I?

JONAH: I'm homeless. I'm hiding. I'm on the run. I'm a liar and a coward.
God is gonna kick my ass if He ever..

SHEILA: You're fucking nuts, and you know what? I don't care.

JONAH: Look, give me your phone number. Once I'm safe in Tarshish, I'll call you sometime.

SHEILA: I don't believe in sometime.
I'm broke, driving a stolen car, and I'm offering to sleep with a lunatic.

(*Silence between them*)

SHEILA: Say something else.

JONAH: One time...not this time, another time...

(*Ballroom dance music, from a distance*)

JONAH: I went down to my stateroom, below C deck. In the distance, I could still hear the music from the ballroom.
(*He's in his stateroom aboard the Carnival Princess. He has a bottle of whiskey, takes a drink.*)

Senor Jose Cuervo turns me invisible. God hasn't
found me. Not yet.
Maybe this time, no fucking thunder, no storm, no
praying…

(The PIRATE QUEEN *comes into the room, without
knocking.)*

PIRATE QUEEN: Hello, Slick.

PIRATES: *(O S)* Yo ho! Yo ho!

JONAH: The Pirate Queen.

PIRATE QUEEN: You remembered. How sweet.
I'll leave the door unlocked, just in case.

JONAH: In case what?

PIRATE QUEEN: In case one of us gets nervous, and
wants to get out.

JONAH: Do I look nervous?

PIRATE QUEEN: You look like a man in a total panic,
despite the alcohol. I'm not sure if its me, or something
else…
(She tosses off an item of clothing.)
In any case, fear looks good on you.

*(They embrace, tear at each other's clothes, fall onto the bed,
or the floor.)*

(Whitecaps, flying fish. A gasp or two. Or three)

MR BONES: Hoo! Hooo!

(The lights dim on the PIRATE QUEEN'S *violent lovemaking.)*

(Music)

*(MR BONES and his backup group of female PIRATES dance
smoothly across the stage, as the lovemaking continues. They
sing, with excellent doo-wop moves.)*

(Suggested song: Nite Owl)

(MR BONES and his fellow songsters disappear.)

(In the bed on C deck, all is calm. Of course, the PIRATE
QUEEN *smokes. So does* JONAH.*)*

JONAH: Its a bad prophecy job. In the end, God will
have mercy on the Ninevians…

PIRATE QUEEN: Ninevites.

JONAH: That's them. They'll repent for a few days,
God will forgive them, and then they'll get back to all
their low life criminal shit, slaughter of the innocents
included.
No one gets punished for their sins but me.
So I'm fleeing.

PIRATE QUEEN: Fleeing, you said? Fleeing?

JONAH: Yeah. Fleeing. From God. His wrath.

PIRATE QUEEN: Really? Isn't that sort of…idiotic?

JONAH: Not at all. I'm heading for Tarshish. A K A
the Big Rock Candy Mountain, buzzin' of the bees,
peppermint trees, that paradise at the end of the world
where I'll be hidden from God forever.

PIRATE QUEEN: Aren't you forgetting something?

JONAH: What?

PIRATE QUEEN: God is everywhere.

(Sound of thunder, soft)

JONAH: Holy shit. Thunder. You hear it?

PIRATE QUEEN: I'm not deaf.
(She starts to dress.)

PIRATE QUEEN: Tarshish is the end of the line. The last
stop. If we get there.

JONAH: What do you mean, *if* we get there?
Where are you going?

(More thunder)

PIRATE QUEEN: Storm's up. I better check our course and speed.
And the lifeboats.

JONAH: Lifeboats?

(PIRATE QUEEN *tosses on some more clothes, heads for the door.)*

PIRATE QUEEN: You're sweet, you know.
I'll be back, soon as I can. Don't stay up for me.

(PIRATE QUEEN*'s gone.* JONAH *staggers out of bed, takes a drink from his bottle.)*

JONAH: I'll get there. I know. Know why I know? I think I've already been there. Over and under, uphill. Down dale. Or was I on the way there…

(*Huge crash of thunder. Seawater pours through an open porthole. Jonah takes another swig.)*

JONAH: Belfry, Joppa, ship, storm, sleep…belfry ship Joppa storm sleep belfry…ship…slee….

(*The Porsche, and* JONAH *reels over into it, falls into a drunken sleep on* SHEILA*'s shoulder, snoring.)*

(SHEILA *drives on into the night, sings to herself.)*

SHEILA: (*Sings. Suggested song:* Nite Owl. *Continuing under:)*
JONAH: (*From dreamland)*
Hooo! Hooo!

(*The song ends.* JONAH *snores.* SHEILA *drives.)*

(*The house by the sea.* MR RHODES *alone. He's silent for a long moment. Then he stands, takes a few hesitant steps.)*

(MR RHODES *talks to himself, and to the air.)*

MR RHODES: Whence comest thou? What is thy country? Great wind into the sea and of what people art thou?

(MARY MARGARET *and* DABBY *come in.* MR RHODES *clearly notices them.*)

MARY MARGARET: Jesus. Jonah again. And again.

MR RHODES: And he said flee unto Tarshish unto them, and was tempestuous against them wherefore they cried unto the Lord…
(He falls silent. He stands there blank.)

(MARY MARGARET *leads her father to his chair. It isn't easy.*)

(DABBY *sit down at the laptop.*)

DABBY: *(Reading off laptop)* Is the brain modular? Does it consist of encapsulated domain specific modules of information—speech center, smell center, vision center, memory core? Or is it an undifferentiated complex neural network, where everything connects to everything else?

MARY MARGARET: Dabby, I have no idea. And I don't fucking care. I can't even get him to…

MR RHODES: Went down into it that we perish not and they said call upon thy God we pray thee perish not.

(Finally MARY MARGARET *is able to settle her father in his chair.)*

(A long moment…)

MARY MARGARET: Dabby, what happens if we forget all the names for things?
If everything we've been taught, all the boxes we put things in, all our ideas about what can be and can't be—if everything we know and believe about the world disappears—as the neurons die.
What happens then?

DABBY: I don't know, Mary Margaret. I truly don't.

MARY MARGARET: I do.
A world where Jonah can sink down into the sea, and
flee from God, and preach at Nineveh—all at once, and
again and again.
Eternity.
Dad's alone in there.
Dad? Talk to me. Please. Say—I know you're with me,
Mary Margaret, and that…

MR RHODES: The ship was like to be broken the
mariners were afraid if so be that God will think upon
us O sleeper arise.
(He stands.)
O sleeper arise.
(He looks emptily around, and sits again.)

MARY MARGARET: Dabby, are you learning anything
actually helpful? One treatment that works.

DABBY: There's no pill for this.

MARY MARGARET: Is there anything new, any…

DABBY: You know what brain neurons hate more than
anything, Mary Margaret? Blood. Its poison. Some of
his left brain neurons drowned in blood. The survivors
need to learn to do all the stuff the dead ones did.
Until they do, he'll be having this Jonah scramble
conversation with himself.

MARY MARGARET: Tell me the truth, Dabby. No lies.
Will he ever get better?

DABBY: Your dad's a brilliant man. His neurons are
clever little bastards. They'll learn what they need to
learn. He's coming along. Feeds himself as well as I do.
The neurologist said he was on course, that it just takes
time for the brain to rewire itself.
He's gonna be all right.

MARY MARGARET: Will he be just like he was before?

DABBY: I'm sorry Mary Margaret, but they never are.
Stroke victims.
As he comes back, some dead circuits get left behind…
an old memory, an old fear. He might make new
connections while he's rewiring himself…sharper
sensations, feelings. New abilities.
Might be subtle.
Might be just fine. You might not even notice.

MARY MARGARET: Shouldn't he be getting better faster?
Be more in touch with the world? With us?

DABBY: Every stroke recovery's different.
His memory will be O K, I think. He certainly knows
his damn Bible. He knows you and me.
You know something, Mary Margaret? I think he likes
it. He likes being in there. Circuits all wrapped around
themselves. Hid from everyone. More than anything,
he's gotta decide to step back into the world outside
his head.

MARY MARGARET: He's with Jonah in there, the work of
a lifetime, dreaming it all, over and over.

DABBY: So—we need to lure him out.

(DABBY *picks up "Toad On The Road". He hands it to*
MARY MARGARET.)

DABBY: *Toad On The Road.* Again.
Its like the Book of Jonah, but there's fewer words.

(MARY MARGARET *takes the book, shows it to her father.*)

MARY MARGARET: Toad on the Road.
(*Reading*)

I love to drive
I am a toad.
Here I come—
Toad on the road.

Hello, cat.
Dad, can you say that?
Hello, cat?…. Cat?

(No response from MR RHODES, *though he seems as if he's paying attention.)*

MARY MARGARET: Hello, Cat, hop inside
I will take you for a ride.
Cat is hungry, stop for lunch.
Sip and slurp. Chew and munch.
I see Pig, on the bus.

MR RHODES: Pig.

MARY MARGARET: Dad, that's good. Good. Pig.
I see Pig, on the bus,
Get off, Pig, and come…

MR RHODES: Get off, Pig!

MARY MARGARET: Get off, Pig
And come with us.
That's good, Dad. Repeat after me.

Drive them here
Drive them there…

(No response)

MARY MARGARET: Drive them here
Drive them there…

(No response)

MARY MARGARET: I can drive them anywhere.
Dad? Dad?

DABBY: Mr Rhodes, trying to help someone who gives
up is like feeding medicine to the dead. You don't want
your daughter doing that.
You gotta try.

(MR RHODES *looks at* DABBY, *and then at* MARY
MARGARET. *He stands up, with effort. Then sits back
down.*)

MARY MARGARET: He won't give up. I won't let him.
He wants us to find him. I know it.

DABBY: So do I.

(DABBY *hugs* MR RHODES.)

DABBY: He's my man.

(*The Porsche, with* JONAH *and* SHEILA. *Screech of brakes,
and she pulls over.*)

SHEILA: This is it.

JONAH: Joppa! I gotta get…

SHEILA: Not quite.
But we made it to the ocean. That's Professor Rhodes'
house, the man I came to see.

(*They get out of the Porsche.* JONAH *takes his bottle.*)

SHEILA: Lights are on. He's home.

JONAH: (*Taking a drink*) I'll get there. I been there before.
Joppa, ship, storm…
I like you. A lot.
I'm telling you everything.
Pray for me.
I was at the rail of the Carnival Princess…

SHEILA: Jonah, just shut up.
Please.
Now I intend to get some folding money from my
friend inside. Why don't you go look at the moon over
the sea, and when I…

(JONAH *looks* SHEILA *over.*)

JONAH: You're pregnant.

SHEILA: You noticed. I didn't think it showed.

JONAH: When are you...

SHEILA: Go look at the moon.
I'll come get you when I'm done.

JONAH: Gimme my car keys.

SHEILA: No.

(SHEILA's gone, toward the house. JONAH staggers off
toward the beach with his bottle. He drinks in the moonlight.
Sound of surf, gulls. MR BONES appears, with a metal
detector.)

MR BONES: Hoo! Hoo!

JONAH: Uh, Mr Bones? You live around here?

MR BONES: Of course I do, Jonah. I live right here.

JONAH: Which way's Joppa?

MR BONES: Joppa? It's a ghost town now. The piers are
rotted away. Nobody home.

JONAH: You're kidding me. I need to...

(The metal detector beeps, and keeps beeping.)

MR BONES: Extraordinary things are hidden down
below. Ancient...
(He drops to the sand, digs. While digging)
...artifacts...secret...antideluvian...chthonic
wonders... Ah!
(He comes up with a small coin. He feels it carefully.)
Fucking dime.
Let the sea have it.
(He tosses the coin into the ocean.)
You were saying?

JONAH: I wasn't saying anything. I was thinking...
Where the fuck am I this time?

MR BONES: On the beach. A fairly famous biblical
scholar lives over there—but he's had an accident. No

use visiting, his conversation ain't what it used to be. Better to stay on the Carnival Princess. You're at the rail, looking out at the sea. Rough weather. A gibbous moon, *(Pointing up)* like this one.

(People in deck chairs with blankets appear. So does the rail. In one deck chair, MR RHODES, movements erratic, head lolling at times, watching JONAH.)

(The people groan and moan.)

MR BONES: Seasick. Pity. *(Laughs)*
Enjoy the cruise.

(JONAH steps to the rail of the Carnival Princess, looks out at the waves a long moment.)

MR BONES: In fact, I'll join you.
(He joins JONAH at the rail.)
But I must apologize for intruding on your contemplations.

JONAH: Please. No intrusion at all.

MR BONES: How good of you to say so. How little kindness there is in the world today, how little thought for others.
May I ask how far you're going?

JONAH: Tarshish.

MR BONES: Beautiful city. Beautiful.

JONAH: Is it? I've never been…

MR BONES: You realize, my friend, that the Dalai Lama is quite correct. If only men would live as brothers, loving each other, seeing only the beauty all around them.

JONAH: What about child molesters, Mr Bones? Rapists, murderers, sleazy landlords, corrupt politicians, judges on the take, racists, sexists, thieves, lawyers, and all the other examples of human stupidity, greed, and pitiless

cruelty.
Do you love them?

MR BONES: We're you ever an actor, Jonah?

JONAH: No.

MR BONES: I was. In my youth. A brilliant actor.
Every actor knows that to play an evil person, you
don't believe you're evil.
You're noble. Misunderstood, a helpless slave to
certain dark parts of yourself.
A victim.

JONAH: What about a city like Nineveh, where the
whole place is a sewer...scum who prey on each other,
day and night? Should we live as their brothers?

MR BONES: Even the lost citizens of Nineveh may also
have their part to play in the great whirl of being and
non-being, of justice and...

(Huge crack of thunder, lightning. The ship rocks.)

MR BONES: Aquatic turbulence. Minor.
Nothing to worry about.

*(The ship lurches crazily, and the deck chairs slide across the
floor. Their occupants scream. More thunder)*

PIRATE CREW: Yo ho! Yo ho!

(The PIRATE QUEEN *enters.)*

PIRATE QUEEN: We have a problem. As I mentioned in
a previous scene, I've thrown the Captain and all the
officers overboard. My pirate crew..

PIRATE CREW: Yo ho!

PIRATE QUEEN: Shut up! My pirate crew are completely
unfamiliar with the workings of a ship like this one.

PIRATE ONE: Its all fucking computers!

PIRATE TWO: The engine room is flooded!

PIRATE ONE: Port bulkhead leaking!

PIRATE TWO: Fire in the hole!

PIRATE ONE: Fire in the hole!

PIRATE QUEEN: If the storm keeps up, and it will, we're all going down together.
Pray—to whatever gods you believe in.

(*Chorus of prayers from the deckchairs to Jesus, Ganesha, Buddha, the Baal Shem Tov, and whoever else their occupants happen to believe in.*)

JONAH: Uh, the storm is happening because of me. God is angry with me. For disobeying his commands. That Nineveh business. Skipping out on the prophecy job.

(*Thunder, lightning. Huge waves crash on deck!*)

JONAH: Throw me overboard!!
Save yourselves!!

(*People in deck chairs moan and keep praying for deliverance.*)

PIRATE QUEEN: This is the core problem of choice in moral philosophy. Either my pirate crew and over one thousand praying passengers, including thirty-four children and six babes in arms, all drown horribly in the freezing depths of the sea. Or I get my own hands bloody and toss him over the side.
(*She looks at* JONAH.)

(*He's silent.*)

(*Thunder! The storm at its peak! The ship tilts and sways!*)

DECK CHAIRS: We split! We split!

MR BONES: Save us all!
Chuck him overboard!

PIRATE QUEEN: I'm sorry, Slick.
Say hello to the sharks for me.

(*The* PIRATE QUEEN *throws* JONAH *into the sea.*)

(He screams! Splash!)

(The ocean immediately calms. The ship stops rocking. The sun shines.)

MR BONES: Good choice.

PIRATE QUEEN: No. It wasn't.

MR BONES: But you saved all these people, and babies, and…

PIRATE QUEEN: Shut the fuck up, you blind bastard, or I'll cut your nuts off and throw you in after him.

(The ship's orchestra strikes up. The people in the deck chairs rise, toss off their blankets and dance.)

(In the sea. JONAH)

MR BONES: Meanwhile, in the sea, Jonah's falling… Down down down, past jellyfish, jars of marmalade, pods of dolphins, down down down…

JONAH: A narwhal!
A buick!
The Marie Celeste!

(The great shadow of the whale appears.)

MR BONES: Leviathan!

(And looms.)

MR BONES: And a great fish swallows Jonah—
Into the belly of hell.

(Darkness)

(In the house by the sea. DABBY, MARY MARGARET, MR RHODES in his chair, no expression on his face. His eyes are still empty.)

(SHEILA is there.)

MARY MARGARET: Go ahead, Sheila. He won't bite. Talk to him. Not too loud.

And repeat yourself. A lot.
And look at him.
He's wounded, not stupid.

MR RHODES: The ship was like to be broken. The mariners. The mariners were afraid…

(*And silence*)

SHEILA: I'm Sheila.
You remember me? From your Old Testament class.

(*On hearing* SHEILA's *voice,* MR RHODES *stirs, becomes more focused.*)

MR RHODES: Do you have soup? Split pea.
Toad on the…hello, cat.

SHEILA: We were dating, sort of…

MR RHODES: I know you. You were very kind.

SHEILA: That's one way to put it.
Is he understanding me?

MARY MARGARET: He's never done this well before.

DABBY: Keep talking to him. Please.

SHEILA: Uh, I need some help from you. I've got a little problem here…

MR RHODES: Do you know any songs?

SHEILA: I know a lot of songs.

MR RHODES: Sing to me.

SHEILA: Later. Maybe later. Right now I want to tell you something.

MR RHODES: Sing to me now.

SHEILA: Do you know me? I'm Sheila.

MR RHODES: Sheila.

SHEILA: That's right. Sheila.

MR RHODES: Of course.

Forgive me, Sheila.
I've been ill.
Do you want something from me? Anything I can give you, its yours. Take anything you please.

MARY MARGARET: Thank God.

MR RHODES: I love you, Mary Margaret.
I missed you.

(MARY MARGARET & SHEILA sing. Suggested song: Diamond in My Crown)

(The song ends.)

(In the WHALE)

MR BONES: Jonah's in the whale; above the whale, on his back, is a bull, on the bull's back an angel, and the angel carries our world on his shoulders. Below the whale is the ocean, and below the ocean, darkness.

(A conversation)

WHALE: Do you enjoy the taste of squid?

JONAH: I never tried it.

WHALE: Delicious. Help yourself. Should be a few tentacles floating around in there.

JONAH: Did you swallow me just by chance, just something to eat, or…

WHALE: Not at all. I don't eat men. They're stringy and tasteless.

JONAH: Then why did you…

WHALE: I'm God's messenger.

JONAH: No. No you're not. That's me. What I'm supposed to be.

WHALE: I'm God's messenger. It's not an exclusive position.

JONAH: Every wino on the corner, every tree flapping in the breeze, every damn flower. Every child that dies young. They all say the same thing. I'm God's messenger. No, I'm God's messenger. No, I'm…

WHALE: Shut up, little man.
My brain is fifty times the size of yours, ten times as old, intricately fissured. Thoughts filter through the circuitry for centuries. And you presume to argue with me, Lord of the Pool, King of the Dip?
I am God's messenger.
Special Delivery.

JONAH: O K.
What's the message?

WHALE: You're here, aren't you? Safe inside me. You're not rolling in the trough of the waves. Dead, ladies and gentlemen! The prophet Jonah, the unfaithful servant, drowned in the deep.
His eyes are blue driftglass.
You're saved. That's the message. Hang up the phone. Relax.

JONAH: Relax? I'm in the belly of hell.

WHALE: Be careful what you say.
You're getting the ride for free.
Let me tell you two stories—one of love, and one of battle.

JONAH: Tell on. I'm not going anywhere.

WHALE: Harpoon guns on factory ships hold explosive charges. When one hits, it blows a hole five feet wide in your side and hooks you deep. You leak your life's blood into the sea as you're dragged close for killing. The Brink of Extinction is not a good place to be if you're looking for love. I am a sperm whale, Physeter Macrocephalus. I spent years, Antarctic seas through the Indian Ocean, and north to the Arctic Circle,

without meeting another of my kind.
Then one night in the South China Sea I surfaced and smelled her, the faintest touch on the wind. I raced through the waves. It took three days and three nights until I found her off Okinawa. She was waiting for me. Do you know what mad love is, you little men?

JONAH: Some of us do.

WHALE: Body to body we dove, and breached into the sunlight off the Azores! Dove and breached again!
She swam away one day, without looking back. I don't know why.
Does this ever happen with men and women?

JONAH: All the damn time. And it hurts, down in the blood, and through and through you.

WHALE: So it does.

(A silence between them. The deep thrum of the WHALE's *heartbeat.)*

WHALE: What color is the sea?

JONAH: Green? Gray? It looks differently depending on…

WHALE: The sea is black. Go down—no sunlight penetrates beyond twenty fathoms. Below two hundred fathoms, where I often hunt, the sea is endless night. You can't even see your own flukes.
Squids are fast and clever bastards. This giant specimen of Architeuthis lived in a cave along the sea bottom, near the Gilbert Islands. I hadn't eaten for weeks, and I went deeper into the blackness than I ever had before. I heard a tentacle slipping out to feel around for food. I grabbed it in my jaws and hung on. It took hours to haul his entire wiggly body out of the cave, and then he tried to kill me. He wrapped his tentacles around me, tore at my skin and flesh. The great battle raged for three days in total darkness. In

the end I bit his head in two. I ate his eye and beak
first. He was tasty down to the gristle.
I still have the scars.

MR BONES: Jonah prays to God for his release from
Leviathan's belly.

JONAH: I swear that if I ever see the sunlight again, I
will be your prophet until the day Death takes me.

(In the WHALE, *swirling darkness)*

(Song: Lord Have Mercy on Me*)*

JONAH & CHORUS:
Lord, have mercy on me,
Lord, have mercy on me,
Lord have mercy on me

Now, is the needed time,
Oh now is the needed time
Now is the needed time

Lord, have mercy on me
Lord, have mercy on me
Lord have mercy on me

(The Great Regurgitation)

(Huge strange sound of the WHALE *throwing up* JONAH*)*

(Sudden light of the shore)

MR BONES: Before he knows it, Jonah is on the beach,
his mouth full of seawater and sand.

*(*JONAH *coughs up seawater, heaves a fountain up.)*

JONAH: God be praised for my salvation from the sea.

(The house by the shore. MR RHODES*)*

MR RHODES: The deep belly of hell. That's where I've
been. My hair's turned white.

I was inside and outside at once. Part of me didn't
want to return to this world. And I understand Jonah
so much better now. The truth of it...
Jonah was a man fated to live the same story over
and over again through the centuries. God's order to
preach, flee, ship, storm, whale, prayer, Nineveh, and
then God's explanation of it all, which Jonah never
understands, and over and over again.
His memory of it all is only fragments.
The journey is always new.

(SHEILA *walks along the beach to* JONAH.)

(*The Porsche is nearby.*)

JONAH: What happened in there? Did you see that
professor?

SHEILA: I saw him.

JONAH: What did you...

SHEILA: I came out here to get the money for an
abortion. The baby's his.

JONAH: An abortion. That's what you want to do?

SHEILA: He's a sick man, my professor. They say
he's getting better, but he's not the man I knew. He's
broken.
I thought I loved him, once upon a time.

JONAH: You get the money?

SHEILA: Yeah. I got the money I wanted. And more.
I don't know.

(JONAH *takes a drink from his bottle. Then he notices—*
SHEILA's *in tears.*)

JONAH: I could, you know, help you out. With a baby.
If I ever get free from God's...

SHEILA: I don't want to hear this. Not now, anyway.

(JONAH *gently wipes* SHEILA's *tears away.*)

SHEILA: Thank you, Jonah.
I'd give you back your car keys, but you're still too drunk to drive.
Get in the car. I'll get you to Joppa after all.

JONAH: I'm not so sure I want to go there.
Let's just rest here on the beach.

(JONAH *and* SHEILA *sit next to each other on the sand.*)

(*Surf, gulls*)

JONAH: Sheila, God came to me again. Uninvited, as usual.

(*Angelic background singing*)

(GOD *appears in the moonlight, searching for* JONAH.)

GOD: Jonah! Jonah!

JONAH: *(To* SHEILA*)* Can you give us a minute?

(SHEILA'*s gone.*)

GOD: Who was that?

JONAH: Sheila. She took my car, and I was…

GOD: JONAH!

JONAH: Yes, Lord.

GOD: The people of Nineveh are poisoned by need, whipped on by fear. If a woman is hungry, she steals the bread from her mother's table. Or rips the lollypop out of the mouth of her own child. If a man is frightened, he fires an automatic weapon into a crowd, slaughters people like cattle, and reloads as they fall.
Check yourself out.
In your mind.
You're as much a thief as the poor sucker who stole the Brinks truck in downtown Nineveh last night, and took a bullet in the head for his trouble. It's only your good luck you haven't murdered or raped anyone yet.
The Ninevians, Ninevites…whatever. Throwing

children into Nergal's belly, hoping that brainless bull
will give them joy. Or peace.
They don't have clue number one, don't know their
right hand from their left.
Desires, hatreds, loves.
They're slaves, bound in chains of fire.

JONAH: Is there no mercy for those poor people?

GOD: Mercy?
They swim in the river of my mercy as Leviathan
swims in the sea.
Do what needs to be done.
Say what needs to be said.
(He points in a direction.)
Nineveh is that way. Start walking.
Remember, Jonah. Tell them.

JONAH: Tell them what?

GOD: All things shall be opened as sure as you knock.
Forty days. Or forty nights. Whatever.

(JONAH starts walking.)

GOD: *(Calling after him)* Time is winding up.
There will be no hiding place. They'll all DIE.

(DABBY's beach shelter in the dead whale's bones.)

*(MARY MARGARET's brought a picnic. They eat and drink,
and the surf rolls…)*

DABBY: You're a very, very beautiful girl, Mary
Margaret, but you're stupid.

MARY MARGARET: Can't say anything nice without
spoiling it, can you Dabby?

DABBY: It's the truth.

MARY MARGARET: Don't be an asshole. I'm not stupid,
and you know it.

DABBY: And yet—you waste your time with a loser like me—a college drop out, a beach bum, a pill head when I can get some, your father's Mr Fixit, an ex-convict…

MARY MARGARET: Come on. You did two months in some kind of juvie hall for stealing a car. You were fourteen.

DABBY: I'm not joking.

MARY MARGARET: Should I find myself a rich old man?

DABBY: A rich young man. Someone with a job. Someone who'll go somewhere, and take you with him.

MARY MARGARET: I can take myself anywhere I like, thank you.

DABBY: Do you think, Mary Margaret, that I've got plans to do something tomorrow besides watch the sun come up, drink coffee, and hunt for driftglass?

MARY MARGARET: The blue ones are the eyes of drowned sailors. And the red ones are…

DABBY: You're not hearing me, Mary Margaret, and I can't speak plainer. As long as you keep coming around, I can't say no to you, and I can't keep my hands off you.
You can do a lot better.

MARY MARGARET: You want to get rid of me.

DABBY: That's not it.
But once your Dad's all better, I may leave this place. Go somewhere new. Find work. Go back to college. I'm just trying to…

MARY MARGARET: You think I'm a mermaid, can't get too far from the sea or I'll die? You think I'm gonna be here forever.

DABBY: I just…
Mary Margaret, I'm only…

MARY MARGARET: I'm going home. I'm calling Beach
Patrol, have them haul away these whale bones, your
whole little seaside shack.
To the dump.
Gimme my sandals.

(DABBY *picks up her sandals.*)

(MARY MARGARET *slowly stretches out one leg, puts her
foot in his lap.*)

MARY MARGARET: Put them on for me.

(DABBY *tosses the sandals at her.*)

(*She laughs.*)

(*Thunder*)

DABBY: Let's get in under the tarp. Its gonna rain hard
in a minute....

(MARY MARGARET *looks up at the sky. They get in under
the tarp, close to each other.*)

(*Rain*)

(*Alone on the beach, the* CASHIER GIRL *looks at the waves.*)

(*Her cellphone rings.*)

CASHIER GIRL: Hello? ...I went out to the beach...
What do you think I'm doin', Bobby? I'm looking at the
ocean. Getting my feet wet. Calms me down inside.....
When do you leave? ...That's soon, that's really soon...
I know about the Army Rangers. My cousin Jed was in.
That's one hard outfit, Bobby.....
I know. I know. I didn't tell my Mom yet, but I'm going
to, soon as I get home.... I don't want you there. You
know what my Mom thinks about you... I still think its
so fucking dumb. And it makes me fucking furious at
you. I'm gonna need you, and the baby's gonna need
you, and you'll be dead.....

I know. I know… O K.
Once I talk to my Mom, come see me. Behind the Dairy
Queen, those tables. Maybe nine, half past nine…..
Bobby, you better be there…
Love you too.
(She hangs up, wanders off, kicking at the sand. She's gone.)

(Nineveh. NINEVITES. JONAH. NERGAL, *a bull with a
thousand eyes.)*

JONAH: Coming in to Nineveh. A pack of dogs tears
at my jeans. Oil slick burns on the surface of a pond.
Floating in a drainage ditch is the corpse of a young
woman, duct tape over her mouth. So dark in the
bottom of the world, the snakes don't have eyes.
Everyone worships Nergal.

(The citizens of Nineveh worship NERGAL, *in their way.)*

(Dance. Chanting. Music. The dance ends.)

NINEVITES: See the sights!
Maps of Nineveh!
Visit the Rubber Room!
Spare a dime, Mister?

*(*MR BONES *appears.)*

MR BONES: Jonah! It's me again, your friend Mr Bones.
Welcome to Nineveh.

NINEVITES: Want to party, sailor?
I'm a licensed guide!
Private dungeon, Mister?
Want my sister? She's a virgin.
Good luck. You'll need it.

*(*JONAH *steps up onto a rise of ground.)*

JONAH: People of Nineveh!

NINEVITES: What? What'd he say?

JONAH: I know how hard it is sometimes to live in
peace with your neighbors.

NINEVITES: Who the fuck are you?

JONAH: I know how hard it is some days to feed those
children who depend on you. I know how hard it is to
find a little warmth in this world.

NINEVITES: Asshole! Go home!

JONAH: How hard it is to find even a splinter of
happiness. How hard it is to love God.
This is not an all-night party. This is not a circus or a T
V show. I am not an entertainer.
This is a rescue mission. I am not gonna ask you to
leave if you're a drunk, or a drug addict, or if you
smoke dope. I am not gonna ask you to leave if you're
a whore, or a thief. I'm not gonna ask you to leave if
you're running from whatever law they got here, or
from yourself.
I will never turn anyone away.
You ever hear of the children of God? His precious
babies. You wonder who they could be?
Every one of you.
And if you're God's child, and he feeds you, and
clothes you, and puts a roof over your head, and gets
you born in the U S A, and gives you the gift of being
able to open your eyes and see the beautiful colors of
the sky, what are you supposed to do in return?
Steal bread from your mother's table? Gorilla old ladies
in the parking lot at the QuikStop? Make a living on
your back at the Traveler's Inn? Abuse children? Rape?
Kill? Generally fuck up?
Hear the word of the Lord. I will burn your chariots
in the smoke, and my sword shall devour your young
lions. The gates of the rivers shall be broken, and the
palace drowned. Faceless men with machine guns
will kill anything that moves, even the dogs. Burning

trashheaps, saltpits, desolation. The cormorant and the bittern lodge in the broken windows, their shrill cries pierce the night. Jackals roam the courtyards and feed on corpses. Ashes in the wind. Nineveh, that great city, will be laid waste, and no one will remain to mourn her passing.

(Suggested song: Why Don't You Live So God Can Use You?)

JONAH & MR BONES: *(Sing)*
Why don't you live so

God can use you?

Anywhere, anytime
Why don't you live so
God can use you, anywhere Lord
Anytime.

Why don't you think so
God can use you?
Anywhere, anytime
Why don't you think so
God can use you, anywhere Lord
Anytime

Why don't you walk so
God can use you?
Anywhere, anytime
Why don't you walk so
God can use you, anywhere Lord
Anytime

Why don't you sing so
God can use you?
Anywhere, anytime
Why don't you sing so
God can use you, anywhere Lord
Anytime

(Song ends.)

JONAH: Forty days. Nights. Whatever.
That's all you get.
Be kind to everyone.

MR BONES: Very well done. But useless.
In the end.

JONAH: How do you know?

MR BONES: Ah. Like yourself, I've been here before.

(MR RHODES. *He's up and walking, and he steps out and looks at the sea.*)

MR RHODES: And the Ninevites cover themselves with sackcloth and ashes, and roll in the gutters in their fever for penance, and whip themselves, and beg to be spared. And God's mercy falls on them from heaven, cleansing the whole city in a gentle rain. And after a month of sackcloth and ashes, the Ninevites forget God and his prophet Jonah, and go again about their business—lying, cheating, raping, murdering and fighting one war after another. Worse than they were before. And you can once again see the neon of Nineveh twinkle from as far away as a neighboring star.
And Jonah?
This time, for reasons as hidden as those for choosing His unfaithful servant in the first place, God allows Jonah to step off the wheel.
There are other prophets, false and true, to tell the people of Nineveh how to live.

(DABBY *and* MARY MARGARET. *She has a suitcase. He has a backpack. Both are dressed up, ready for travel.*)

(MARY MARGARET *is wiping tears away.*)

DABBY: What did your Dad say?

MARY MARGARET: Nothing.

DABBY: That's a lie. We said all our goodbyes to him, and then he called you back. He must have…

MARY MARGARET: He just said, God speed you, Mary Margaret.

DABBY: That's all?

MARY MARGARET: Then he cried and kissed me and cried again. And I cried too. And then he said, you and that young man go make your way in the green world. Fair winds.
And call me every Sunday.

DABBY: I'll remind you.

MARY MARGARET: I won't forget.
Not ever.

(They're gone.)

(MR BONES on the sand. JONAH approaches with SHEILA.)

JONAH: Mr Bones?

MR BONES: Ah! Jonah.

JONAH: This is Sheila.

MR BONES: *(Kissing her hand)* Delighted.
You'll have a beautiful baby.

SHEILA: Thank you.
Haven't I seen you at the Grass Skirt?

MR BONES: Maybe. I get around.

JONAH: What are you doing here?

MR BONES: I could ask you the same question. Cruise liners are at the docks in Joppa. A storm is gathering on the horizon. The noble citizens of Nineveh still pray to Nergal, and feed him their children.
And you hang out on the beach, with a lounge singer.

JONAH: I wouldn't put it that way.

MR BONES: How would you put it?

JONAH: My part is done. God won't call on me again.
It's over.

MR BONES: So it is. The Book of Jonah is finished. Toss
it on the fire.

SHEILA: Where's Mary Margaret? And Dabby?

MR BONES: The shack made of whale's bones is empty.
They're gone. Out into the world.
They were only waiting for Mr Rhodes to be well
enough.
I told you, Jonah, that I was once an actor. My eyes
worked well enough back then. My first theatrical
venture was with a troupe of community theater
rejects bringing the Bard to the boondocks. We're in
Chump Junction, playing The Tempest. I'm backstage,
in costume as Trinculo. The audience began to throw
things. Gunshots rang out. I peeked onto the stage. A
local theater critic had opened up with a twelve gauge.
Prospero and Miranda were bleeding all over the set.
I ran out the stage door behind the theater. We had an
old mare who'd been taught to dance. She'd cross her
feet when she walked if music played. The Waltzing
Horse. She was tied to a post, munching grass. I rode
her, bareback, off into open country. When I got about
a hundred yards off, I looked back. The theater was on
fire. I kept going all night till we hit a highway, right at
a small strip mall. I rode that horse into the parking lot.
It must have been around six in the morning. Between
Hong's Chinese Take Away and a Nail Salon was a
music store with a speaker mounted over the door.
It had been left on all night, and I could hear a slow
bluesy tune. My horse began to dance a stately waltz
across the empty parking lot. I slid off her back, went

over to the road to hitchhike. I left her dancing there alone as the sun rose. For all I know, she's dancing still. Time is winding up. Live while you can.

(No one moves. Sound of the surf. Fade to darkness)

(Dim light on the PIRATE QUEEN *alone, on her knees in silent prayer.)*

PIRATE QUEEN: *(Sings softly)*
Lord, have mercy on me,

Lord, have mercy on me,
Lord have mercy on me.

Now is the needed time…

(And continuing under…)

MR BONES: The carnival cruise liner, saved by the sacrifice of Jonah, sailed on toward Tarshish. Piloted by pirates, she hit the rocks off Okinawa. A gaping hole was torn in her hull. She sank into the sea. Every soul on board, including six babes in arms, was drowned. Or eaten by sharks.
Except the Pirate Queen.

PIRATE QUEEN: I floated for two days and nights, hanging on to the roulette wheel from the ship's game room. On the third day, more dead than alive, I came ashore on this small island. I lay on the sand, too weak to move, as the surf washed over me.
I was rescued by the nuns who live here, separate from the moving world, in a stone abbey by the sea. I spend my time in prayer, asking for understanding, and forgiveness.

MR BONES: Often, at night, when the moon shines through her window, the Pirate Queen remembers Jonah, and she sees his face, looking up at her as he sinks beneath the waves.

PIRATE QUEEN: *(Sings softly)*
Go down, you blood red roses, go down

Go down, you blood red roses, go down
Oh, you pinks and posies…

(Music)

(The Grass Skirt Grill. The Love Tones are onstage.)

BAND MEMBER: Aloha.

*(JONAH and MR BONES at the bar. MR BONES finds his
drink, a Zombie skullpuncher, and says to no one at all…)*

MR BONES: Beautiful night. A gibbous moon.
Is Sheila onstage yet?

JONAH: She'll be out there in a minute.

MR BONES: Thank you.
Jonah, isn't it?

JONAH: Yes, it's me.

MR BONES: Do you ever think of the Pirate Queen? She
loved you, you know.

JONAH: Sometimes, late at night, I think of her.

MR BONES: So do I.

JONAH: Let me buy you another one of those. *(Calling)*
Wanda?
WANDA: You callin' me?

JONAH: Another Skullpuncher for the gentleman.

MR BONES: Thank you again. Kindness is rare enough
in this world.

(Music. The band plays. SHEILA appears onstage.)

(Suggested song: You Belong to Me)

(The song fades, along with the Grass Skirt Grille.)

(MR RHODES *alone in his house by the sea.*)

MR RHODES: I am a citizen of Nineveh, covered with sackcloth and ashes.
(*He lights a candle, and once again takes up his Biblical researches.*)

(*Distant thunder*)

MR RHODES: The Book of Jonah, with its four chapters and 231 verses, is inexhaustible.
The gourd vine, the great fish, the cattle, the ship, the sea...
My work on it has barely begun...
A long silence. He studies his books and papers...

(*The* CASHIER GIRL, *alone behind a Dairy Queen, somewhere in America. Moonlight in the trees. She dials her cell, listens to a brief message, then leaves one.*)

CASHIER GIRL: Bobby? Where the hell are you? I been waiting almost two hours. The Dairy Queen closed an hour ago. Everyone went home. They turned out all the lights, even the neon sign. You know the one, says Softserve, Super thick. Queenburgers. Chili Fries.
Bobby, we gotta talk.
I can deal with you going in the army. I can.
We'll make it work.
I'm not giving up this baby, and I'm not leaving it with my Mom. No way.
You know what? They got housing on army bases for families. I looked it up. We could come along.
I'm sitting in the dark on one of those picnic tables.
Bobby, it's creepy back here.
If you don't show up soon, you
son-of-a-bitch, I'm going home.
(*She hangs up. She stands, looks up at the sky, paces, then sits back down at the picnic table.*)

(From the darkness, MR BONES *appears.)*

MR BONES: Ah, we meet again.
(He holds out to her an open box of candy.)
Jujubee?

*(*CASHIER GIRL *hesitates, then take one, pops it in her mouth.)*

(Moonlight)

(From the dark around them, everyone appears.)

CAST: *(Sings)*
Above, I heard, is where we go

Above, they say, is where we go

Along the starry path we go
Along the Milky Way.

Above, I heard, is where we go

Above, they say, is where we go

Along the starry path we go
Along the Milky Way.

MR BONES: Go to sleep, kids. Pleasant dreams.
Hooo! Hooo!

(From somewhere high above, an OWL *answers.)*

OWL: *(O S)* Hooo! Hooo!

END PLAY

AFTERWORD

Toad on the Road is by Susan Schade and Jon Butler, a Step into Reading book, Step 1, from Random House, 1991.

Suggested musics for songs:

You Belong to Me — Jo Stafford, Kate Rusby, others

Diamond in my Crown — Patty Loveless, Be Good Tanyas

Blood Red Roses — traditional sea shanty, many recordings

Nite Owl — Tony Allen and the Champs, Genya Ravan

Lord, Have Mercy on Me — from Daniel in the Lions Den, Bessie Jones and Group

Why Don't You Live So God Can Use You — Corey Harris and Henry Butler, Muddy Waters, others

Above I Say — words Len Jenkin, music is roughly a slowed down *Merrily We Roll Along*...

Suggested musics for dances:

The tracks, or played live by a band:

Carnival Cruise Line boarding:
Sadagora Hot Dub — Amsterdam Klezmer Band,
Shantel remix

In the Ballroom:
Bossa Nova Baby — Elvis Presley, youtube remix for
Astaire-Hayworth dance

In Jonah's stateroom:
Nite Owl — Tony Allen and the Champs

Entry into Nineveh:
Adir Adirim — Balkan Beat Box

For underscoring, as always

Santo and Johnny

www.ingramcontent.com/pod-product-compliance
Lightning Source LLC
Chambersburg PA
CBHW070026110426
42741CB00034B/2624